ANIMAL

First published in 2003 by Oberon Books Ltd.
Electronic edition published in 2012

Oberon Books Ltd.
521 Caledonian Road, London N7 9RH

A catalogue record for this book is available from the British Library.

PB ISBN: 978-1-84002-393-0
E ISBN: 978-1-84943-852-0

Cover photography: Manuel Harlan

Photo Montage: Jai Redman

eBook conversion by Replika Press PVT Ltd, India.

for Peter Carr with love and thanks
and
The Women In Black

Of all tyrannies a tyranny sincerely exercised for the good of its victims may be the most oppressive.

C S Lewis

Production Notes

The set of *Animal* must incorporate three surveillance cameras.

The surveillance / security camera images used in *Animal* must be projected over the entire performance space and performers.

When Pongo remembers it is usually at the very moment of speaking – and not anecdotal. It is active not reflective.

In production, Elmo's stand up comedy act would be further devised and developed with the actor and director.

Animals or Angels?

We are living through extraordinary times. Earlier this year, two million people marched in London against a Labour government's drive to barbaric war. There was direct action at army bases, school strikes and widespread spontaneous acts of protest. There is a growing public disillusionment with British institutions and a demand for greater levels of democracy and accountability.

Animal was commissioned and written before this explosion of dissent, but in the parallel universe of the play an ongoing war is taking place, against which there is a wave of mass protest. Charting the relationship between these protests and an experiment on a man expressing anti-social behaviour, the play raises vital questions for our time. What constitutes anti-social behaviour in an inhumane society? Should anger be socially managed / controlled, or is it a vital component of our humanity?

Animal centres on an anger management drug trial (with military interests) and raises fundamental questions about the ethics of human experiment. Most human vivisection takes place in the 'third world' or on vulnerable people, such as Pongo, in the West. The poor, the mentally ill, prisoners and soldiers top the list of 'volunteers' in poorly regulated drug trials. The recent horror stories from Nigeria and Thailand clearly expose the inhumanity of this 'scientific progress' – children given placebos are allowed to die. In *Animal* 'treatment' turns to torture. Many treatments in the West are, in a sense, pharmaceutical experiments. For example, Gulf War syndrome is a side-effect of a medical try out; anti-depressants such as Prozac and Zoloft (the long-term effects of which are completely unknown), are prescribed on a mass scale to a trusting public.

The Chemical Weapons Convention of 1992 prohibits the development of any chemical for warfare that can 'cause death, temporary incapacitation or permanent harm'. Shockingly, it is permissible for a state to develop and use such

4

chemical weapons on its own population – for riot control or crowd dispersal for example. With the war on terrorism, and the inevitable occupations, the lines between warfare and suppression of a state's dissenting population may become blurred. The idea of non-lethal weapons (an oxymoron) is gathering support amongst politicians and the military. It is also an emerging market for the pharmaceutical companies who seem quite content for their products to be weaponised. Many of the calmatives currently in development are derived from the same chemicals as Prozac and Zoloft, others from Valium. Ketamine (ecstasy) and Rohypnol (date rape drug) are also being used.

How should theatre respond to such global developments and to the scale of political events since September 11? There has certainly been a resurgence of art activism on the street and perhaps because truth is at such a premium, a renewed interest in factual interrogation. The most artistically exciting explorations at present seem to be participatory / democratic in form or, rarely, like *Animal*, wild epic dreams which seek to free the imagination against the status quo and offer a pro-found ethical questioning of humanity at a crossroads. Perhaps we are moving, finally, into a new age of public theatre.

Kay Adshead is a poet, a visionary. In *Animal*, the government closes the park to anti-war protesters; there are school strikes; calmatives are being developed; a man kills a swan for food. In 2003 this unlikely combination of events have all been headline news. It is this struggle to see patterns in the chaos of our world that makes Kay's work so vivid. *Animal* is set in an alternative reality, but it is clearly about our reality now. It appears far-fetched, one version of events, but it is also actually happening. It is an extraordinary and complex work which raises disturbing philosophical questions about how we move forward into the new Millennium.

Will we be Animals or Angels?

Lisa Goldman
Artistic Director the Red Room
August 2003

Animal was first performed at Soho Theatre on 4 September 2003 with the following cast:

Dr Lee   Fiona Bell
Elmo   Mark Monero
Pongo   Richard Owens

Director   Lisa Goldman
Designer   Soutra Gilmour
Lighting Designer Chahine Yavroyan
Sound Designer   Matt McKenzie
CCTV   Owen Oppenheimer
Music   Patrick Tenyue
Press
Representation   Emma Schad
Photo Montage   Jai Redman

For The Red Room
Artistic Director   Lisa Goldman
General Manager   Michael White
Writing Associate Sarah Dickenson

PART ONE

1

Midsummer – at the centre of a London park a stone's throw from the Strand – a beautiful house.

It is a treatment centre.

A blackbird is singing. Far away the sounds of a happy crowd – a military brass band – celebrations.

Sitting in the sunshine – a large man in his seventies, and a younger woman in her thirties, casually dressed, they both appear relaxed, almost sleepy.

PONGO: I love brass bands.

DR LEE: Yes?

PONGO: They're cheerful.

DR LEE: Are they?

PONGO: Of course they are. I love the euphonium.

DR LEE: I can't think what a euphonium sounds like.

> *Pause. PONGO does an uncanny impression.*

PONGO: I love the tuba.

DR LEE: You don't think it's…ridiculous.

PONGO: Of course!

> The trombone.

> *PONGO does an impression.*

> And the trumpet.

DR LEE: Everyone likes the trumpet.

Pause.

PONGO: What do you think of cornets?

DR LEE: Cornets?

PONGO: Yes. What do you think of them?

Pause. PONGO does an impression of a cornet.

DR LEE: *I don't like them.*

PONGO: Neither do I.

They laugh. A pause.

DR LEE: You must be tired. It's been a long day for you.

PONGO: It's been a wonderful day.

Pause.

Who was she?

DR LEE: (*Smiling.*) Don't you know?

PONGO: Yes, yes. I think I do.

DR LEE takes a mug of hot chocolate and puts it to his lips, he drinks, and with a napkin she wipes his mouth.

DR LEE: Do you want to stay sitting here and watch the sun go down?

PONGO: I'd love that.

She gets up and stretches.

Do you eat when you get home?

DR LEE: Yes.

PONGO: Your other half rustles something up for you.

DR LEE: Sometimes.

PONGO: Sometimes you eat out.

DR LEE: (*Laughing.*) Not often now.

PONGO: He wears…white.

Slight pause.

DR LEE: I like him in white.

PONGO: He has short, black hair that curls into his neck.

Slight pause.

Blue eyes,

and a broad manly chest.

DR LEE yawns.

He has a broad manly chest?

Slight pause.

But babies are tiny things.

DR LEE: Yes.

PONGO: Who does she look like?

Pause.

DR LEE: She looks, just like herself.

PONGO: What's it like…to be a mother?

Slight pause.

DR LEE: It is wonderful and terrifying.

Far off a cheery brass band.

PONGO: Are they still marching?

DR LEE: Probably.

PONGO: And, overhead, are the planes saluting the…
generals?

DR LEE: Yes.

PONGO: And the admirals, and Their Majesties.

DR LEE: Yes, we saw the planes.

PONGO: Did everyone have the day off work?

DR LEE: Nearly everyone.

PONGO: Did they cheer and lean over the barricades and wave their flags?

DR LEE: (*Smiling.*) Yes, they did all that.

PONGO: And it snowed bus tickets.

She tries to tuck in the blanket over his knees, he flinches and whimpers.

DR LEE: (*Softly.*) People touch each other. You must try and get used to it.

She smiles.

Now don't stay up too long, Peter. I don't want you to catch cold.

She makes to go.

PONGO: I LIED.

There are three surveillance cameras. One clicks and whirrs as it follows DR LEE. A pause.

DR LEE: Did you?

PONGO: Yes. I lied to you.

DR LEE: What about?

PONGO: What do you think it was about?

DR LEE: I think it was about…

PONGO: Brass bands? That's right. I hate brass bands.

Military brass band, furious marching tune, drum, cymbals, the works.

CCTV projected over performance space, grainy surveillance / security camera footage.

PONGO (the patient) is filthy, dirty, unkempt and naked. He is squealing, screaming, hurling chairs, table and papers. In blurry foreground is another figure trying to calm him down. The picture flickers, the sound quality is poor, competing with the brass band only one word in ten is heard.

In anguish PONGO is banging his head over and over in time with the big bass drum.

Silence and blackout.

2

A torch shines into PONGO's eyes. He hasn't moved from Scene One.

ELMO: *(Recognisable as the shadowy figure in CCTV.)* Knock, knock.

Pause.

PONGO: Who's there?

ELMO: Derision. Derision room for da two of us in dis town.

He is holding a half-eaten hotdog in paper and a can of lager, he giggles, he is pissed.

PONGO: She forgot about me.

ELMO: Who?

PONGO: The Bosnian lady with the ring through her nose.

ELMO: Doc'll go apeshite.

ELMO pulls down PONGO's eyes.

PONGO: I didn't get my last shot.

ELMO: Tongue.

PONGO pokes out his tongue.

Say 'red lorry, yellow lorry'.

PONGO: (*Tongue still out.*) Red lo, red l... Why?

ELMO: 'Cos it cracks me up.

ELMO starts to eat his hot dog.

PONGO: Gimme a bit.

ELMO: Mitts off.

PONGO: Oooh! I didn't get my milky drink. I didn't get my Jammy Dodger.

ELMO: (*Scoffing, laughing.*) Pongo's sweating on his J D.

PONGO: Will you get my shots, Elmo?

ELMO: Day off, mate.

PONGO: Will you get my tabs?

ELMO: I haven't got the keys.

PONGO: (*Getting agitated.*) The walls'll start to breathe.

ELMO does heavy breathing.

I'll spit maggots.

PONGO / ELMO: (*Together.*) Spiders'll crawl out of my arsehole.

ELMO: (*Hot dog finished, slurping back lager.*) Come on.

PONGO: What?

ELMO: We'll tell her to open the drugs cupboard.

PONGO: She scares me.

ELMO: Who?

PONGO: The nurse. Her eyes are full of suffering.

ELMO: She's got piles. Come on.

PONGO: In a minute.

ELMO: Come on.

ELMO initiates a play fight.

PONGO: In a minute.

PONGO is much stronger, he pushes him off.

IN A MINUTE.

ELMO collapses chuckling, puts fingers to lips to Ssssh.

I love you Elmo.

ELMO: What?

PONGO: I…

ELMO: I heard.

PONGO: You do a gig tonight?

ELMO: I don't do Thursdays mate. Thursday is try out
scum. I do Fridays!

PONGO: Where have you been?

ELMO: Over the park.

PONGO: Who are all the people?

ELMO: They're Protestors.

He puts his nose to the air, wafts a scent to him.

Smell that.

PONGO puts his nose to the air.

Pussy.

PONGO: Pussy?

ELMO: There's fresh pussy spread out all over the grass, political pussy, with placards, pussy for peace.

PONGO: Did you…?

He giggles.

ELMO: Nearly, Pongo old man, nearly, gave an agitating young lady the soft Elmo eye, she'd pitched right by the lake.

PONGO: Not near the swans?

ELMO: Cracked on I was a little brother of the tee pees, she invited me in for a pow-wow, dead hospitable.

In posh female voice.

Dandelion tea? Sprouting alfalfa bap? Gave me the old rabbit on collateral damage. I agreed to work for The Future of World Peace if she let me lift up her cheesecloth; fingers getting a Niagara going down there, her toes are starting to crisp nicely, when this gorilla calls out,

(*Camp voice.*) 'Oh Gabby I can't get my pole in straight,' just as mine was about to go in good and straight, know what I mean, so come on, I've got to go back out: see, demonstrate solidarity with the sisters, I've got knob ache.

PONGO stands.

PONGO: Something happened today.

ELMO: Don't feel you have to share it with me.

PONGO: I'd been with the Doctor talking, my heart started to pound, my mouth was dry and I kept… blinking…I couldn't stop blinking, my arms and legs were heavy, but inside my head my brain was like a light bulb, and somebody had just flicked the switch, and I saw a great brick wall and standing in front of the great brick wall was a woman, a nice little woman shaking out a red and white table cloth billowing like a sail, and the sky was so blue, and fluffy white clouds raced, and it snowed breadcrumbs and the air was full of sparrows.

You know what that was, Elmo?

That was… Memory.

3

ELMO: For a mile there's nothing but blackness and the Park trees, then in the moonlight you see shapes, like molehills and then you're picking your way through legs and heads and it's all

'Sorry mate' and

'Excuse me darlin.'

Further out towards the lake they've pitched camp and lit fires, and I mean that is trouble, 'cos you can't do that, I mean take it from me, no way can you do that, and the bodies are standing up now and it's like

'Heh, we're a crowd, trying to get somewhere; trying to put one foot in front of the other.'

'Cept you can't 'cos there's more bodies in front of you – and more bodies are coming up behind all the time, mostly mums with babies in buggies, the odd bloke with a kid on his shoulder – and we're starting to press against each other, like we're a squashy mass, and some sick joker takes it on himself to sway, just a bit from the knees, and this starts a ripple and the crazy people are laughing and you think well that's all right until some poor fucker falls down and gets his brain stamped on, and you look up and there's bodies in the trees and a mad girl is waving like...

'Back. Go back.' (*He demonstrates.*)

and people think she's being friendly and it's

'Yoo-hoo.'

Way off I can hear the crackle of loudspeakers.

'Do not leave the Park. Make no attempt to leave the Park'

and the stamp of horse's hooves. Then suddenly we stop, like we're going nowhere, we're stuck, and I'm rammed against this little redhead, knocking on, but with these heavy, soft, pendulous breasts middle-aged women have, that really do it for me, and they're squashed flat against my chest and I can smell her tea rose armpits and I mean my Percy Thrower's standing straight out – like digging into her thigh and I know it, and she knows it but we're being all English about it and I smile and I say

'What's up?'

which is not the right thing to say 'cos we both know what's up alright and she laughs, and she's got her own teeth and she says

'They've closed the Park Gates, they won't let us out'

and I say

'Why?'

and she says

'They think we're going to link up with the crowd outside the Ministry of Defence'

'That's an infringement of my civil liberties'

I tell her, thinking I'd like to take a few civil liberties with her if there were a tad less people about.

And they're chanting 'Stop The War' and it's ear splitting.

We're about two hundred yards from the gate and my back's against a Park sign, and I turn around and put my arms around and shin up it. I can see the Riot Police on the other side of the twiddly wrought iron gates and I eyeball this twat on a big, black, steamy equine number and I shout, trying to be heard over the crowd.

'Hey mate, I've just had a call, my wife's having a baby'

…but it's hopeless …so I swivel round, find my ID from my trouser pocket and I wave it and bellow.

'I'm not one of them, I work in the Park'

and I'm about to tell them who for – when this kid, maybe twelve, thirteen, who's been climbing the gate gets to the top, shouting, something like

'Mum, mum'

and he's going to jump down when one of the cops at the front whacks him with his electric cosh and the kid screams and falls down like a swatted fly. And that was a mistake 'cos in a jiffy there's fifty shinning up the gate, a hundred, two hundred and the cops' truncheons are bashing and poor fuckers are dropping to the floor and moaning

A small baby crying in distress.

and then some big butch bastard on our side shouts

17

'One, two, three, Heave!'

and everyone pushes at the gate and people are falling over and getting kicked and screaming 'one, two, three, heave'

and before you know it the fucking wrought iron gates, twenty foot high with spikes on the top are starting to lean forward, just ever so slightly and the riot police bring the horses closer so their noses are poking through the railings and their nostrils are flaring and steaming and, the horses' red eyes look wide and scared and they're stamping and spitting and foaming and then there's a snap and a buckling and a section of the gate crashes forward and all you can hear is this terrible screaming like I've never heard before. A spike has pierced the horse's eye, gone right through and out through the cheekbone and blood spurts like a fountain and the horse is screaming and the crowd gasp and I feel a gush of hot blood on my lip and I feel sick and the horse tries to rear up, it's hooves strike the air and the fucking spike's still stuck in it's eye and the rest of the gate starts to slide down bringing the horse to it's knees and behind it the other horses scream and rear and spit and snort and all the crowd; kids and mums are being trampled by the thrashing hooves and their cracked, yellow teeth are bared and biting and frothing, and I can't forget their soft, lolling tongues and their huge mad rolling eyes.

Baby suddenly stops crying.

4

DR LEE in white coat. ELMO in white nurse's uniform – both have discreet Pharmaceutica insignia on the pockets.

PONGO is seated centrally. He has shaved his beard, changed his hair. He is clean and smart.

PONGO: I'm getting better.

DR LEE: What does that mean?

PONGO: It means I'm not being angry.

DR LEE: Were you angry a lot?

PONGO: I was always very angry.

DR LEE: What made you angry?

Pause.

PONGO: Well...

DR LEE: Try and be truthful Peter. You mustn't make things up to be amenable.

PONGO: No.

Pause.

Well, I'd washed my smalls in the Gents by The Reading Room and I was discreetly drying them on the radiator in Modern Classics when this posh bloke, with a baldy head, complained to the desk lady and he was very loud about it, you know, disturbing all the other readers; very uncouth. It was disgusting he said, making the library smell like a ruddy latrine, I was disgusting and I was embarrassed because I knew the desk lady for years; and she always let me dry my smalls on the radiators in Modern Classics on a Monday; and she had to call the head librarian and he doesn't like her on account of her migraines and I suffer from the occasional migraine myself and I was really very angry indeed because I was banned then and I had nowhere to dry my smalls and I liked it in the library and I had to stop reading.

DR LEE: What did you do then, when you were feeling so very angry?

PONGO: Well…I waited.

DR LEE: Yes…?

PONGO: I waited till the posh bloke with the baldy head came out of the library and he saw me and he called me filth…human filth and that made me very, very angry so I hit him, I hit him, in the head.

DR LEE: You hurt him?

PONGO: I hurt his head.

DR LEE: And sometimes you hit people just for looking at you.

PONGO: I can't remember that.

DR LEE: And sometimes you stole.

PONGO: Yes, I stole food and watches and chocolate to give to ladies in the Park shelter and I stole a park bench and put it under the railway bridge, but that was a borrow, and twice I threw bricks at banks to steal money, and I ate dog dirt in front of the Morning Smile café when they stopped me going in because they said my trousers were shitty, and I used to wee on people when they slept.

DR LEE: Street people?

PONGO: Yes.

DR LEE: I see.

PONGO: And people at bus stops, I used to wee on them.

DR LEE: You did that when you were angry?

PONGO: Yes, sometimes when I was angry, sometimes when I wasn't angry I did that!

ELMO looks pointedly at PONGO.

Pause.

DR LEE: You said you're getting better.

PONGO: Yes, I can think.

DR LEE: Couldn't you think before?

PONGO: I stopped being able to think...because of the drink and sometimes because of the cold.

DR LEE: Explain to me what not thinking is like.

PONGO: It's quite painful.

DR LEE: Yes?

PONGO: It's like being lost, being lost in space. Yes, it's like floating about in space in a space suit.

DR LEE: What is thinking like now?

Pause.

PONGO: It's good.

DR LEE: How is it good?

PONGO: Well, before, when I was thinking; before, I'd get stuck and just think about the one thing over and over... say...I'd think about, well, sitting on the tube and this woman moving away and I'd think about that all day and night and the next day and night. I'd think about it for weeks and months, maybe years, just that, but now I'd think, well, perhaps she was frightened or perhaps she just had to get off at the next stop...see I'd think more about what *she* was thinking and that's different.

DR LEE turns and looks directly into camera...a brilliant smile. DR LEE speaks into camera.

DR LEE: Eleven.

She looks at watch.

11:40, twenty-second June.

Peter.

She turns to him.

You like the name Peter, do you?

PONGO: I love it.

DR LEE: Peter has now been in the Centre four and a half months.

PONGO: (*Shyly, into camera.*) Five.

DR LEE: Sorry?

PONGO: I've been here five months next week.

DR LEE: Do you know, that's spot on.

Into camera.

Peter has been at the Centre five months.

I'm going to show this tape to my colleagues.

PONGO: You do that every week.

DR LEE: And they are all very impressed with you, Peter.

PONGO: They won't send me away, will they?

DR LEE: What do you mean?

PONGO: Away from here?

Slight pause.

DR LEE: We hope, very much, one day you'll leave here

and go back out.

PONGO: What will I do?

What will I do Elmo?

ELMO: (*Gently.*) I don't know.

PONGO: What do people do when they leave here?

Slight pause.

ELMO: They go home, mate.

PONGO: Oh.

DR LEE: Maybe there's someone out there. Someone you've forgot.

PONGO: No, no there was only... Mam, always...

He remembers, it is hard for him.

You see

a stork brought me, I remember I had a picture of it, it wore a jaunty sailor's cap and held me by my napkin in its yellow beak.

DR LEE: At the moment you're sleeping fifteen to eighteen hours a day?

PONGO: I brought a lot of trouble on her.

DR LEE: That's right, isn't it Elmo?

ELMO nods.

PONGO: 'Cos her family were God-fearing.

DR LEE: We want to cut that down...

PONGO: Mam didn't believe in God. God is the good that lives in human hearts she said.

DR LEE: We want to cut that down, so in two to three

months you might be sleeping nine to ten hours.

PONGO: More time to remember.

DR LEE: Yes, I suppose you could say that.

PONGO: You don't like me remembering.

DR LEE: Of course, I like you remembering. So with your permission we are going to slightly change your medication.

PONGO: Yes.

DR LEE: You might find yourself getting a little agitated sometimes, it won't last long, you mustn't worry about it.

PONGO: I don't want to wee on anyone.

DR LEE: We'll keep a very close eye on you and we'll make sure you know what's happening next.

PONGO: This is a next, is it?

DR LEE: Yes, Peter.

You might get the odd headache, dry mouth etc... But we can give you other medicine to help that, do you understand... You might have a few toilet difficulties.

PONGO: I don't want to wee on anyone.

DR LEE: We won't let that happen.

Pause.

Do you have any questions?

PONGO: Yes, where am I, again?

DR LEE: You're in a small residential treatment centre in London.

PONGO: I thought I was in the Park.

DR LEE: Yes, the Centre's in the Park.

PONGO: Who are you?

DR LEE: I'm Dr Lee. I am a psychiatrist and this young man likes to be called Elmo, and he is a psychiatric nurse.

PONGO: I'm mad then, am I?

DR LEE: No, Peter, I do not believe you are mad.

She takes his hand. PONGO allows it to be held for a second then pulls away.

But you have been ill, probably for a great many years. We need to get you sleeping less and then it would be nice to set you some small tasks...would you like to help in the kitchen?

PONGO: Killing chickens?

DR LEE: No...no, we have our own small vegetable patch, perhaps you could take over that.

PONGO: I don't think so, thank you. I don't like vegetables. Do you have chickens?

DR LEE: No...no chickens.

PONGO: You can eat swan.

DR LEE: Yes, but that wouldn't be very nice, they're nicer to look at, aren't they, swans?

PONGO: They're nice to look at and they're nice to eat.

DR LEE: Anyway, in time, we'll find something for you to do.

PONGO: I'd rather just think, thank you.

DR LEE: You can think and do things, Peter.

PONGO: At the same time?

Anxiously.

Another next.

DR LEE: You're feeling overwhelmed right now, but we will help you, we will help you take one thing at a time.

PONGO: Really, I just want to remember.

DR LEE: Of course you do and that's fine for now but it's not the most important thing.

PONGO: We built a scullery snowman, Mam and me… and he was a brother, husband, father…

DR LEE: We are hoping to significantly improve your motor skills.

PONGO: And she gave me two bits of coal, a carrot and a comb…

DR LEE: Can you write Peter?

PONGO: And he was smiling at the mangle, smelling my stew and staring at me with his black coal eyes…

DR LEE: We know you can read beautifully.

PONGO: And the stew bubbled and the snowman melted and I was glad 'cos I thought he might be a German.

DR LEE moves away making notes on her palm top. ELMO stands in the middle.

Mam went to work at the bomb factory and they tried to make her file the pointy bit at the end, but she couldn't sleep, she said, thinking of the kiddies she'd be blowing up, they hadn't made no war, she told the men, so they moved her to the works canteen making counterfeit custard, and women pointed at us in the street and someone posted dog dirt and wrote Conshie on our back wall.

ELMO: He's recovering more early memories every day.

DR LEE sighs.

Isn't that what you want?

DR LEE: (*Still making notes.*) It's nothing to do with what
I want. We mustn't forget that Peter is on the study
because we're trying to treat his behavioural problems.

PONGO: But Mam, who had black boot polish hair and
merry green eyes (*To DR LEE.*) you have soft black hair
and brown eyes, said never mind, and I played jazz
trumpet for the starlings.

DR LEE: I'm going to go away, Peter...

PONGO: And Mam danced in the parlour with Mr Fred
Astaire.

DR LEE: ...and match a development schedule to your
medication.

PONGO: And even the cat learnt to Jitterbug.

DR LEE: (*To ELMO.*) We are looking for a steady
improvement in the quality of Peter's day to day life.

PONGO: And everything that happened in the world
ended up cut into neat squares hanging on a rusty nail
in our carsey, we wiped our bums, we wiped our bums
on it, we wiped our bums on it Mam and me.

PONGO is crying.

Can I ask a question?

DR LEE: (*Gently.*) Of course.

PONGO: Why've they closed the Park?

5

ELMO: The twiddly Park gates are gone, with their iron
peacocks and lions and coronets and wild rose. There
are these ugly great wooden jobbies now, reinforced

with steel girders and barbed wire, they open to let cars in, and there is a little sentry box entrance at the side.

I'm not supposed to use the gate from inside the Park, but Fridays I do my gig and everything has to be – just so – I shit, shower and shave, put on my lucky, Mona Lisa's fanny, boxer shorts, black shirt, Versace strides, Gucci shoes, have a double scotch on the rocks and then I'm out of there, past the lake; chuck the Tunacrap sandwiches to the swans, across the Park, the long way, going over a new bit in my head in my head, that's how I rehearse.

Flash the ID.

'Shouldn't be using this gate'

'Sorry pal'

then out into the traffic and the lights.

On the street side the wooden gate is covered in flowers, when they wilt people come and put others, they nail them to the planks, there are also photos, some laminated to stop them spoiling in the rain, and a great sign which says 'two million dead' with pictures of dark eyed children and a smaller sign written in scroll which reads 'Martyrs for Peace' and has photos of the British kids. There's mementoes, teddy bears, fluffy bunnies, poems people have written, bibles and cards, and also, and this really does my head in, clothes splattered in blood, from that night. There's a tiny hand-knitted cardy with bloody cuffs, and a shoe with a bloody lace...

...cops are a permanent presence. No one's around the gates, but across the road there's a vigil of about one hundred people, day and night.

At the very front, sat in a deck chair, like she's on Brighton beach is the mother of one of the kids trampled to death by the horses.

She's young and might have been a bit of a looker, but she's shaved her head and she's very thin now. Around her about twenty or thirty weird looking birds all dressed in shabby black. The press call them her handmaidens, which is a bit sick since she lost both of her hands that night. I don't know if she received medical treatment I suppose she did, but she's got these bloody stumps wrapped in grimy bandages that she folds in front of her. It's very quiet but her lips are moving all the time.

You can't get close enough to look into her eyes.

CCTV, blurry image, taken from the other side of the road, about twenty or thirty women dressed in black.

6

A week later, sunshine, a blackbird is singing.

ELMO stands restless but good-humoured. He wears a coat and drinks coffee from a paper cup. Throughout the scene, the alarm system is being tested.

PONGO has chunky felt tip pens and a large sheet of paper.

Scattered about are discarded pieces of paper covered in curly writing. 'Happy Birthday', 'Merry Xmas', 'It's a boy', 'Congratulations', etc, etc.

ELMO: I wouldn't have minded if it had been 'Excuse me, sir', 'Thank you for your cooperation sir...'

PONGO: 'Have a nice evening sir.'

ELMO: No friggin' chance; it was...

PONGO: (*Shouting.*) 'Alright, alright. Against the wall. Legs apart. Hands in the air.'

ELMO: Yeah, yeah.

PONGO: Were they cops?

ELMO: No, the…CAF. Puffy bank clerks dressing up to get a hard on.

PONGO: Where'd they take you?

ELMO: Public library. I mean how weird is that, a little back room, piles of old stock books, 'Home Cobbling' and…'Baking without eggs'.

Alarm goes off.

PONGO: After the war Mam worked at the cake factory…

ELMO: Ran a full computer check…

PONGO: They had huge metal tubs, fifty foot high, twenty foot across.

ELMO: This little twat, only looked about twelve, asked me what I thought about conscription.

PONGO: Mam was on top of a big ladder turning a crank that mechanically kneaded the cake mixture.

ELMO: So I told them.

PONGO: Everything fell into that tub she said, spectacles, toupees, buttons…false teeth. She said a man bought an Eccles cake at Salford Market that had a glass eye and a fringe.

ELMO: I told them it fuckin' stank.

PONGO: Fumes from the shrink wrapping made girls more amenable to advances from dispatch…

ELMO: I told them I'd wipe my arse on their conscription.

PONGO: …so Mam put in a request to be sent to hand finishing.

ELMO: Tossers!

PONGO: Icing 'It's a boy' or 'Happy Birthday' and decorating with Palma violet diamonds, marzipan stars or sugar pearls. She found Gertie for me in hand finishing, her speciality was piping, she had two raisins for eyes, a crystalline lemon segment for a smile and... *(Awkwardly he indicates breasts.)* like cream buns.

Pause.

ELMO: Oh, that reminds me.

He takes out a bra from his pocket and holds it up.

PONGO: From your...

ELMO: They throw them to me on stage.

PONGO takes it. He holds it between two fingers.

Frilly, flowery, sporty, underwired, pump cleavage...

PONGO: Pump cleavage?

ELMO: ...halter, strapless, 32A up to 44DD, that's a 32DD. I don't think I've got one of them, I want that back, quite rare they are.

PONGO: What do you do with them?

ELMO: Used to nail them to my ceiling, now they're in piles.

PONGO: *(Handing it back.)* I've never seen...

He indicates breasts.

...never in real life.

ELMO: No?

PONGO: Or...

He indicates down below.

...you see, I've never...had...a woman Elmo.

ELMO: Never?

Are you sure?

PONGO: I'm sure.

ELMO: Perhaps you've had one…and then forgot.

PONGO: Do you think…?

ELMO: Look, really concentrate.

PONGO does so.

And try to remember.

PONGO's face brightens.

Yeah…yeah?

PONGO: No.

ELMO: You poor fucking sod.

PONGO: What's it feel like?

ELMO: Nice.

PONGO: Nice?

ELMO: It feels nice mate, feels like…

PONGO: Yeah…?

ELMO: You're a man, know what I mean?

PONGO: No.

ELMO: Well…

He gathers his thoughts.

…right, I mean you start off with her mouth and it feels…well soft and warm.

PONGO: And damp?

ELMO: Yeah.

He thinks.

Yeah. And then you'd probably move onto her tits…

PONGO: And they feel…?

ELMO: Well like tits…giving them the old 1–2.

PONGO: 1–2?

ELMO: Lick and suck.

PONGO: Lick and suck?

ELMO: And she might be panting, making little thrusts with her pelvis and you might put your hand between her thighs and gently push them apart and you put your tip in first, I mean that's if you are both.

PONGO: Naked.

ELMO: Yeah, and you make sure that she's wet, that's dead important and she likes it, then a bit more, a bit more and you forget about her mouth and her tits and you're shafting away and it's getting quicker and quicker and it's like you're all knob…

PONGO: All knob.

ELMO: And she's all soft silkiness and…you explode.

Pause.

PONGO: Can you repeat that?

ELMO registers PONGO's erection.

ELMO: Filthy fucker.

PONGO: No, no, that was beautiful.

ELMO: (*Surprised.*) Was it?

PONGO: Yes it was. You've got a way with words.

ELMO: Have I?

PONGO: You really have…

Slight pause.

It was like poetry.

ELMO: Yeah?

PONGO: Do you like poetry?

ELMO: No.

Well yeah, yeah. I like poetry.

Pause.

He thinks.

Yeah, I love poetry.

ELMO: What happened with Gertie?

PONGO: Mam wanted me to marry her.

ELMO: Yeah?

PONGO: She wanted grandchildren I reckon, gingerbread ones, but…well, we didn't hit it off.

ELMO: Why?

PONGO: She wobbled.

ELMO: They're supposed to wobble.

PONGO: She'd had too many egg custards.

ELMO: Ah!

PONGO: P'raps she was an egg custard.

Alarm bell goes off.

What's that?

ELMO: Testing a new alarm system.

PONGO: Where's Dr Lee?

ELMO: Out.

PONGO: No, she's in the Centre.

ELMO: You've seen her?

PONGO: I hear the little baby.

PONGO shifts uncomfortably.

ELMO: How's your arse?

PONGO: Burning. If you never did a number two in your life what would happen to you?

ELMO: You'd fill up with shit, till it extruded through your eye sockets, nostrils, your fingernails and your toenails and then a van would come and spread you all over my Uncle Jacko's rhubarb.

Outside a car, then footsteps over gravel, PONGO and ELMO move over to the 'window'.

PONGO: Who are they?

ELMO: Don't you know? They put food on our table, a roof over our heads. They sent me away on that team-building weekend in Woking, they introduced me to asparagus quiche and they introduced you to your girlfriend. They are our very best friends in all the world.

It's Pharmaceutica!

7

Click and whirr. CCTV. Conference table shown from DR LEE's point of view. Men sit around, also a few women. Their faces are not clearly seen. They are watching slides, alternatively they are in light and dark.

DR LEE: (*Standing, addressing audience.*) I believe Peter, as we call him, has the potential for the kind of self-improvement that lifts the TR14 study onto another level of psycho-pharmaceutical achievement.

Here is an elderly man who arrived at the Centre, without identity, without history, barely recognisable as a human being.

He'd lived on the streets for thirty years, maybe more – had carved an existence outside the conventional boundaries of, what we call, normal life – was prone to manic episodes and irrational rage, and was capable of such repellently anti-social behaviour, that police psychiatric social workers had labelled him beyond hope or help.

A damaged and troubled soul, who, for reasons we may, or may never understand, appeared almost as a victim of the twentieth century itself.

She deviates from notes.

I'd just like to say everybody in the study is very taken with Peter, his candour, his unique take on the world, his really quite remarkable assimilation into our family here at the Centre, has actually made me feel quite humble.

She coughs, blushes, back to notes.

Underneath the dirt and damage we are recovering an intelligent individual, complex, sensitive, warm, even talented.

Truly, a civilised man.

8

PONGO: I'm itchy.

Park. A tuffet overlooking the lake. Park bench. PONGO and ELMO are feeding the ducks. PONGO is bundled up in layers of clothes. He has weeping sores the size of postage stamps over his face hands and body. He appears agitated and fidgety. He keeps crossing and recrossing his legs. Over all the scene, the shadow of the swirling birds, and throughout the sound of their cawings.

Can't *you* give me something.

ELMO: No, not this time.

PONGO: Why?

ELMO: You're on a program, a special program.

PONGO: Am I?

ELMO: Yes, your progress is being monitored.

PONGO: Is it?

ELMO: I can't give you anything until I've discussed it with Dr Lee.

PONGO: Why won't she talk to me anymore?

ELMO: She's busy, she's an important lady.

PONGO: Important?

ELMO: She's got other patients.

PONGO: Has she?

ELMO: Mr Dawkins and Elaine and Derek and Pauline.

PONGO: Does she talk to them?

ELMO: I don't know.

PONGO: Are *they* itchy?

ELMO: Look, I can't say.

PONGO: Why?

ELMO: I just can't, mate, that's…

PONGO: Secret.

ELMO: No…no.

PONGO: It's Top Secret.

ELMO: Look.

PONGO: Classified.

   High Risk.

ELMO: Crap!

PONGO: Lips zipped, keep schtum or we'll end up fish food, yeah?

ELMO: For Christ's sake!

PONGO: Why are you red, Elmo?

ELMO: I'm not red.

PONGO: You're upset.

ELMO: I'm not upset.

PONGO: You're angry.

ELMO: (*Shouting.*) I am not fucking angry.

   A bird attempts to swoop, he ducks.

PONGO: Why are you shouting?

ELMO: Shut it, right, just…

PONGO: (*Zipping his mouth shut, through clenched teeth.*)
Knock, knock.

Who's there?

Quacker.

Quacker nuther bad joke and I'm out of here.

He dissolves into fits and giggles.

ELMO: You're perky.

PONGO: It's the drugs.

Pause.

Where are all the people?

ELMO: What people?

PONGO: The Park people.

ELMO: They're not letting them in.

PONGO: Are we the only people allowed in?

ELMO: And Derek and Pauline and Elaine.

PONGO: Not Mr Dawkins?

ELMO: Not Mr Dawkins.

PONGO: I don't like the park without people, it's...

ELMO: Scary?

PONGO: Yeah.

There's a duck with one foot.

Pause. He randomly chucks bread.

Will there ever be people in the Park again?

ELMO: 'Course there will.

PONGO: (*Suddenly distressed.*) I don't think there will. I think there'll only be the birds...we had a flamingo, once, in our back yard.

ELMO: Yeah?

Pause.

You sure about that mate?

PONGO: One summer evening, I was playing jazz trumpet in the carsey and I saw Mam in the scullery door, still as a statue, staring and I looked out and perched on our dirty old brick wall was a flamingo – a real flamingo, with pink knees standing on one leg, the other stretched out behind her, like a ballerina at the bar, and Mam had tears in her eyes even though she was smiling, and they spilled onto her pink, powdery cheeks and that's the only time I ever saw her cry in my life.

Suddenly distressed.

Ooh. I'm itchy. I have to see Dr Lee, now right away.

He starts to pull up his shirt.

ELMO: I'll get you something.

PONGO: See everywhere, everywhere.

ELMO: Back at the Centre I'll sort you out...I promise.

PONGO starts to unbutton his flies.

A bird swoops and pecks ELMO's head.

PONGO: (*Waving arms.*) Go on, clear off. CLEAR OFF.

ELMO: Calm down, mate.

Mopping his bleeding head.

And zip up!

Pause.

PONGO: Will it frighten the beautiful swans?

9

DR LEE and ELMO. On the floor facing downstage, an empty baby carriage and much baby paraphernalia, blanket, clothes, toys etc.

ELMO: He's pining for you.

DR LEE: I'm sorry?

ELMO: He's starving himself.

DR LEE: What about sleeping?

ELMO: He's lucky if he manages eight or nine hours a night.

DR LEE: Really?

She paces.

ELMO: He found a picture of you in the Centre brochure, he masturbates over it.

She stops.

Or is that too much information?

DR LEE: Where?

ELMO: In his room, at night, under covers.

She paces again.

DR LEE: Elmo, what you have to understand, is that I am very ambitious for Peter. I did not rescue him from a difficult but arguably colourful life on the streets, only to see him leave the TR14 study to join a lot of dribbly old men sat in overstuffed chairs watching daytime TV in a toilet of a council nursing home!

She is almost shouting.

ELMO: No one wants that.

DR LEE: Glad to hear it. So it is our fervent desire here at the Centre, desire of the whole team, unanimous desire, that he leaves to take his place as a useful and fully contributing member of society?

ELMO: (*Cautiously.*) Yes.

DR LEE: Good, that's good to know, because I don't mind telling you I will consider anything else an abject failure.

Pause.

ELMO: He misses your talks.

DR LEE: Talking has been useful as a diagnostic tool, but the time for talking has come to an end. Peter's illness must now be dignified by being treated exactly as a medical illness.

Pause.

ELMO: I see…it's just…never mind.

DR LEE: No, spit it out.

ELMO: Well, in my opinion, my professional opinion, he has become quite dependent on what he perceives as your…friendship.

DR LEE: And in my opinion he is at the stage in his treatment program when he must become less dependant.

ELMO: Mm…it's just…mm.

DR LEE: (*Snapping.*) Peter is extremely lucky to be at the Centre…TR14 is ideally suited to the biochemical imbalance, in my opinion, responsible for his past…

rage…and best of all Peter is not having to swallow longwinded wishy-washy gobbledygook from a quack psychotherapist, or analyst, prepared to extract a small fortune from the NHS on behalf of vulnerable patients, like himself, only to tell him that he's disturbed because his hard pressed mother went out to work or his father never played catch with him!!

A baby gurgles in an adjoining room.

Inge's with her.

ELMO: Inge?

DR LEE: She's new, they're getting to know each other.

Baby laughing.

I will have to go in a minute, I'm still feeding.

Pause.

I'm sorry I raised my voice. I'm…upset.

Pause.

I saw a young soldier today…at the hospital who came back from active service so severely traumatised, he tried to smother his young children. His ex-wife called the police. They were planning to prosecute him for attempted murder. Can you imagine? Barbaric.

ELMO: Try and cut down your hours.

DR LEE: I can't. I've NHS patients who've waited two years to see me.

ELMO: Here then.

DR LEE: The work is too important.

Pause.

I spoke to the strange woman at the Park Gates today,

the woman with no hands, have you seen her?

ELMO: Yeah.

DR LEE: I say I spoke to her, actually I spoke at her, I'm really not sure she hears…it's so tragic – her baby must have been about the same age as my daughter. I find it utterly extraordinary that they allow her to sit there day in day out. She's obviously quite ill, she's in deep shock, her wounds might be getting infected. And the police seem so…insensitive. I'm terrified for her.

Pause.

ELMO: I try not to let her get to me.

DR LEE: How's your father?

ELMO: My mother.

DR LEE: Yes, how is she?

ELMO: Oh. She died.

DR LEE: I'm sorry.

ELMO: That's alright, I never liked her.

DR LEE: You were adopted…weren't you looking for your birth mother?

ELMO: No, no. Look p'raps you'd better go and feed your baby.

Pause.

DR LEE: You don't like me very much, do you, Elmo?

ELMO: Like you?

DR LEE: You've never liked me. You find me stiff and unapproachable. You call me The Android.

ELMO: (*He laughs.*) So they're bugging the men's bog now?

DR LEE: (*Slightly flirtatious.*) And it upsets you, it upsets you very much, that a woman is running the whole show here. Be honest with me?

ELMO: No, it doesn't upset me. And; to be honest, I've never really seen you as a woman.

Pause.

DR LEE: (*Suddenly brisk.*) I'm going to prescribe Peter Urecoline – tell him; it's empowering for patients to take an interest in their medication, keep an eye on the blurred vision, he might need reading glasses, oh, and an antihistamine for the skin lesions.

ELMO: I've already done that.

Pause.

DR LEE: I beg your pardon?

ELMO: He was in considerable discomfort. You were not in the building.

DR LEE: But I was at the hospital.

ELMO: You didn't respond to paging.

DR LEE: Well, of course, I turn my pager off during sensitive consultations.

ELMO: I decided it was not…humanitarian to allow the patient to continue suffering.

DR LEE: How many studies have we worked on together?

ELMO: This is our fifth.

DR LEE: Really, five, as many as that. The Alzheimer study stands out to me. I loved the Excellon one. I loved working with those kids, but there was something particularly rewarding and poignant about the Aginon project. Do you remember Mrs Lotsky?

ELMO: Of course.

DR LEE: You know, I still get letters from her daughter.

ELMO: Yeah…?

DR LEE: They managed a holiday this year, apparently…

ELMO: (*Under his breath.*) Groovy.

DR LEE: Five studies and this is your first humanitarian gesture…

Look; we are overseeing a strictly controlled scientific experiment here, we can't have nurses prescribing for patients on a whim, your action might have led to Peter being removed from the study. Normally this would be a disciplinary offence, but of course I appreciate you were acting in, what you thought were, the best interests of our patient so I'm prepared to turn a blind eye. I apologise for my inaccessibility…but I request you never do that again.

Pause.

ELMO: Actually…I can't promise that, if he's uncomfortable I'd do exactly the same thing.

Pause.

DR LEE: (*Coldly.*) Perhaps you'd show me the jigsaw?

They move to the front of the stage and peer over what looks like a large black rectangle.

ELMO: It's the firmament, all the stars, suns, moons, twelve thousand pieces.

DR LEE: He did this himself?

ELMO: In record time, Mensa hype it as the most difficult jigsaw in the world.

DR LEE: With no help?

ELMO: You can check the film.

DR LEE: (*Smiling.*) Extraordinary, I knew his motor skills were improving, but this is spectacular, a major breakthrough in Peter's development, I've always said expert one-to-one nursing is the secret weapon on the TR14 study...

ELMO makes to leave.

ELMO: Oh, and one more thing, Pongo... Peter, has got it into his head the TR14 study is top secret.

Pause.

DR LEE: (*Wearily.*) You seriously think we would want to keep work as important as this secret?

CCTV. Night. PONGO is sleeping in a small cell-like room. The door opens, click and whirr.

DR LEE enters. She stands staring at PONGO in his sleep.

Camera close up on DR LEE's face.

She turns and goes.

10

PONGO is being violently sick into a bucket. He still has the weeping sores.

PONGO: It started with a scratchy feeling when she did a wee. She went into hospital. They cut her open and gave her a bag to wee in, and the house started to smell of the dark, then at last Mam came home, but I knew it wasn't right cos she was always cold and she never got out of bed and we had bed pans and that palaver and she was that ashamed and a nurse had to come, and on the doorstep she said to me.

'You know your mam's not going to get better don't you?'

and I said

'No'

and she said

'Well she isn't love'

and four days later…four days later…

He is violently sick into a bucket.

ELMO: You know, Pongo, I don't think all this talk about your mother's helping you.

PONGO: Four days later…

ELMO: I think you're just upsetting yourself.

PONGO: …her breathing went funny, growly, and then I heard a loud click and her eyes rolled back in her head and…and…she was dead, and I think that was when it started…

ELMO: What started?

PONGO: All the cruelty in the world.

He is scratching his sores.

They're digging holes Elmo.

ELMO: Who is?

PONGO: Round the Park, deep holes with branches over them. No one knows.

ELMO: Yeah?

PONGO: They live there, they come out at night. They sneak into the Centre and steal things, they come into my room, they stand over me. They watch me while I sleep.

ELMO: No one watches you.

PONGO: I'm frightened.

ELMO: Nothing to be frightened of, mate.

PONGO: Oh, there is, there is.

Moon goes behind a cloud, it darkens.

He whispers.

There was nobody at Mam's funeral, only me and
Annie Ezard…and I was so…angry because she had
been a wonderful person…she had worked hard, tried
to be happy and she…loved me, Elmo, so much and I
wanted everyone from the street, the town…I wanted
everyone in the world sat there to hear that this had
been a…wonderful…human being.

And the vicar said 'Lizzie'

no one called her that

'Lizzie,' he said.

'Will be up there now with an egg nog in one hand a
Marlboro Light in the other.'

Well that was wrong 'cos she only smoked at Christmas.

'Watching Mr Fred Astaire, maybe doing a bit of a
dancing of her own, seeing as she was light on her feet'

and I was…very, very angry because they were private
things I'd told him in the parlour the night she died,
and he had no right to repeat those things no right at all
and Mam had been such a…a…very private person and
when the coffin moved back and the curtains started to
pull together…

From ELMO's stand up.

VOICE: (*Off.*) 'Hot foot from the Madhouse'

PONGO: I felt so very, very, angry!

VOICE: (*Off.*) 'It's the Ladies Man himself'

PONGO: And all I could hear was this terrible screaming.

Wild laughter and applause. ELMO lit for his act.

11

ELMO: Now, your full on psychos, I'm talking biting head off baby budgies here, your full on psychos, all have highly polished shoes...honest... I mean I would go as far as to say an early investment in Cherry Blossom virtually guarantees a lifetime amongst the criminally insane, unless you're a Jehovah's Witness.

I nursed a Jehovah's Witness, right, who made it to Broadmoor. He had shiny shoes *and* a bow tie, God's honest truth, that combination is fucking lethal. I mean the mind boggles what you'll find in his deep freeze.

Now, your lady psychos all display a greater than average amount of facial hair, share a fondness for Michael Crawford CDs, and wear those gross slippers that make your feet look like radiated fucking sheep heads... I mean what's that about?

You shag when she's wearing those and it's like you're about to take it up the bum from a pair of Giant Beanie Babies.

Now your retard...or shelf stackers as we call them in the biz...always wear shoes two sizes too big, have long woolly scarves and they have teeth that go in different directions – and that's men and women that is. Why is that?

(*He speaks faster.*) Now, your schizos, they're a particular

favourite of mine they like to vary their appearance –
glass eye in, glass eye out. They take a great pride in
their appearance...you know matching accessories.

'I mean do these shoes go with this bread knife'

Your average manic-depressive loves Gardener's
Question Time.

Your obsessive compulsive, yes I mean you ladies...
has a thong for every day of the year...with the date in
a little heart...twentieth November 2003, twenty-first
November...your religious maniacs masturbate to the
Cardiff Male Voice Choir singing 'All Things Bright
and Beautiful', your kleptomaniac has, at some point in
there life, worked in a hardware shop and I mean we're
getting new disorders in all the time.

Especially the lovely ladies.

Reason defective disorder, this seems to hit the babes
very hard.

(*To audience member.*) Have you got it? Thought so.

Pause.

Why else would you be with him.

No lads there's an easy way to find out if your girlfriend
has this...if she hangs an article of *her* clothing in *your*
wardrobe on the second date she's got it, if she's never
kept a job 'cos she says her boss always wants to get into
her knickers she's got it.

If she shows up at the office Christmas party looking
like Tracy Emin...she's got it.

If she decides to go out and find a coffee at three am
after sex even when it's her house she's probably got it.

And if she gets her cousin, who wants to be a doctor,
to administer a DIY blood test after your first snog, she
definitely has it.

And it's an epidemic, I mean look at the Peace Chics, how many camped there in the Park, twelve thousand. They've all got it, how do I know? They braid their underarm hair. They prefer to poo in the open air. They all have pen pals on death rows and they think Deepak Chopra is a profound thinker.

And Christ, are they ugly! Some of them, I mean alright so Mother Nature hasn't blessed you with natural beauty but you don't have to get your hair cut at The Pet Clinic. Some of them are so ugly when they masturbate they get arrested for cruelty to animals. One of them went for a sex change, the surgeon had to flip a coin…I mean when she took off her bra it looked like she had four big toes and I mean I am the original breast man…no, no I'm sorry that's sexist isn't it girls, alright I'm a breast person…I love breasts…do you know what the little bumps around a woman's nipple are for…they're Braille for suck here.

Do you know a recent survey said you can tell a woman's innermost personality from her bra, I mean, cup size…design, age, the works.

He looks at a woman.

You're wearing a Wonderbra, right?

To man next door.

When she takes it off you wonder were here tits are.

He's distracted by something on the other side of the room.

Yeah?

I think you've seen this act before, darling.

You're a smidge too early.

Don't get me wrong. We all want to see them.

What's this then?

(*To audience.*) Oh, she's keeping it coming.

What?

He looks around as if for help.

You trying to be funny.

Click and whirr of CCTV.

Film. Night. Distant shadowy figure making its way over flat open parkland.

Click and whirr. Another camera picks up the figure approaching the lake. Figure gets closer. It is PONGO, he is naked.

Click and whirr. A third camera...blurry. Close up – a violent frenzy, a strange non-human screaming. A carving knife catches the moonlight.

Blood.

The camera image starts to fracture – cutting out, stopping, starting until it becomes a series of still abstract images ...sound is abstracted, fractured.

Fractured images make a face. A screaming face.

Film judders back into live action.

Sound of a milling crowd, a riot.

Close up. Handless woman at a roadside sat in a deckchair, candlelight.

Close up. She stands...she screams over and over.

12

Milling crowd. A riot.

DR LEE and ELMO.

A dark corner of a London street skirting the Park, in the shadow of large trees.

DR LEE is panting, her cheek is grazed. She is nursing a hurt wrist.

ELMO has pulled her out of the way of the crowd. He is shaken.

DR LEE: I'm alright…I'm alright. Thank you.

> *She looks off.*

ELMO: Don't even think about it.

DR LEE: What?

ELMO: Going back.

DR LEE: Did they rescue her?

ELMO: (*Puzzled.*) Rescue?

DR LEE: The woman with no hands. Did they get her into the van?

ELMO: (*Pause.*) No, no they didn't.

DR LEE: (*Groaning.*) The poor creature.

> *Pause.*

ELMO: I watched you.

DR LEE: You watched?

ELMO: I wasn't sure what you were trying to do.

DR LEE: Wasn't it obvious, wasn't it obvious to everyone I was trying to save that woman's life?

> *Pause.*

Her family are distraught, do you know that? She has a seven year old desperate to get mummy back? Her husband is in clinical shock. She's trying to starve herself to death.

ELMO: The women feed her, I've seen them.

DR LEE: Oh, they hold a bowl of soup to her lips, a cup of water, but they don't get her medical treatment, there has been no attempt to fit her with prosthetic hands, and I really think her wounds might be, gangrenous, when you're close to her the smell is appalling. I had to stop myself gagging.

ELMO: Did she speak to you?

DR LEE: Mmm? She spoke, but she's not…coherent, she's out of her mind, sometimes she imagines she is holding the dead baby it's…heart breaking.

Pause.

ELMO: She made them bury her hands with her son.

DR LEE: What?

ELMO: I read it somewhere.

DR LEE: Some filthy rag…the women again, they use her shamelessly, manipulate her to get maximum publicity.

ELMO: I don't believe that.

DR LEE: If you ask me they *want* her dead.

ELMO: No.

DR LEE: And now people are coming to gawk at her, coach trips even, can you imagine? Bringing candles, trying to touch her skirt, her feet, her wounds even, like she's some sort of religious icon. It's sick.

ELMO: (*With irony.*) Didn't realise you felt so passionately doctor.

Pause.

You shouldn't have done it.

DR LEE: What?

ELMO: Tried to inject her against her will.

DR LEE: You're one of them.

ELMO: No...no.

DR LEE: You'd prefer her to starve to death, to martyr herself.

Pause.

ELMO: But *they* definitely don't want that, do they? They've been trying to break up the Protest for months? They couldn't use force and risk harming the woman so they brought you in, the white coats, 'cept you were in disguise and when talking didn't work, you have no faith in talking anyway, you went for the crafty needle up the bum, but you couldn't pull it off could you? You see never mind her, you're being used Dr Lee.

Sounds of rioting.

DR LEE: They're terrifying.

ELMO: Who?

DR LEE: The...mob.

Pause.

ELMO: You had no right to try and move that woman against her will.

13

A naked and injured PONGO is kneeling and is covered in blood. He trembles. He is holding a large carving knife. In front of him is a mutilated and dead swan.

End of Part One.

KAY ADSHEAD

PART TWO

Click and whirr of CCTV camera, blurred image, kitchen, large stove, three large bubbling saucepans.

Click and whirr, zoom in closer. In one pan the wing of a swan, another the leg, a third the head and neck.

Blackout.

1

PONGO is sat down. DR LEE and ELMO stand over him. A baby is crying…gurgling…laughing…crying from a nearby adjoining space.

PONGO: Why did you stop seeing me?

DR LEE: I have other commitments, Peter.

PONGO: Why did you stop talking to me.

DR LEE: I'm talking to you now.

Pause.

PONGO: Why are there police everywhere?

DR LEE: People got into the Park; the police are there to stop them getting into the Centre.

PONGO: Bad people.

Slight pause.

DR LEE: People who have no respect for other people's possessions or property…people who mistake chaos for freedom…ignorant people who are frightened of things they don't understand

PONGO: Why does Elaine wear a hat all the time?

58

DR LEE: I can't discuss other patients with you.

PONGO: Why am I locked in now?

DR LEE: The door was unlocked as a privilege.

You lost that privilege when you went out and killed the swan.

PONGO: I though it was a next!

ELMO: He thought it would please you.

DR LEE: Peter can speak for himself.

PONGO: (*To DR LEE.*) WHY DON'T YOU LOVE ME ANYMORE?!

He is frustrated, angry, the baby stops. Silence. Pause.

Knock, knock…

ELMO: Come on mate.

PONGO: (*Softer.*) Knock, knock.

ELMO: Who's there?

PONGO: Amish.

ELMO: Amish who?

PONGO: (*To DR LEE.*) Amish you so much.

Pause.

DR LEE: I've shown the other doctors your jigsaw Peter. They were extremely impressed. You're quite a reader now?

PONGO: The Bible, Grimm's Fairy Tales, Gulliver's Travels, Mein Kampf, I've always wanted to read that.

DR LEE: And I believe you wrote a letter?

PONGO: To Mrs Ezard our next-door neighbour, I think

she's dead.

DR LEE: I want you to write another letter.

PONGO: Two letters?

DR LEE: I want you to write to the Park grounds man, he loved the swans…

PONGO: He loved the swan, Elmo.

DR LEE: I want you to tell him how sorry you are.

Baby starts gurgling.

You know killing the swan was wrong don't you, Peter?

Pause.

Don't you?

Pause.

PONGO: Yes.

DR LEE: Why?

PONGO: Because it was beautiful.

DR LEE: We don't kill ugly things either, do we?

PONGO: No, though I'm sure everybody wouldn't have been so angry.

DR LEE: And it won't happen again?

PONGO: No.

DR LEE: Good.

And you will write that letter for me?

PONGO nods.

Baby noises stop.

I want you to start working, immediately, in the kitchen

gardens.

PONGO: I don't like vegetables.

DR LEE: How is the difficulty in urinating?

Pause.

ELMO: Small improvement...but...

PONGO: No...

ELMO whispers something to DR LEE.

Don't...I told you, don't tell her that.

DR LEE: There's nothing to be embarrassed about, it's easily put right.

ELMO: I was surprised at the dosage.

DR LEE: Sorry...?

ELMO: I thought I'd misread it. I asked for it to be formally checked, and noted.

PONGO: The donkey dose, you gave me, he said, Elmo said.

Slight pause.

DR LEE: Elmo is a comedian Peter, we know that... now your other symptoms, dry mouth, constipation, difficulty in urinating and blurry vision are known as anticholinergic, they are annoying but in no way dangerous.

PONGO: Do you forgive me?

Pause.

DR LEE: It really isn't for me to forgive you.

PONGO: Say yes.

DR LEE: (*Softly.*) Of course, I forgive you.

PONGO: Touch me.

Pause.

Please, people touch each other…please.

Pause. DR LEE smiles, she approaches PONGO attempts to put a friendly arm around his shoulder, to pat him, PONGO makes a dive for her, buries his head in her shoulders, hugging her like a huge child. He starts to snivel and sob. DR LEE wishes to extricate herself. She looks to ELMO. ELMO is watching.

CCTV. Blurred images. Early morning. PONGO digging in garden. ELMO watches him. Click and whirr, another camera. A figure of a woman watches them both.

2

PONGO: (*Sat in a chair, he is dictating a letter to ELMO.*)
Dear Swan,
I am sorry I killed your wife. She was very beautiful –
and very strong, she pecked me hard and tried to crush
me with her white wings. I killed her with a carving
knife. I will never forget her.
Yours regretfully,

(*To ELMO.*) What do you call me again?

3

DR LEE sat at a desk. ELMO stands. They are formal.

ELMO: I'm here to express some concerns.

Pause.

DR LEE: Concerns?

ELMO: Yes, some serious concerns.

DR LEE: About the study?

ELMO: Partly, yes.

Pause.

DR LEE: Fire away.

ELMO: I haven't been given access to the outpatient reports.

DR LEE: They're extremely encouraging.

ELMO: I see.

DR LEE: Just get to the point, Elmo.

ELMO: I'm no longer seeing any improvement in three out of ten of the test volunteers.

DR LEE: Really?

ELMO: And questionable improvements in others.

DR LEE: Mr Dawkins was always going to prove a challenge.

ELMO: Elaine concerns me.

DR LEE: She's much calmer.

ELMO: She's not shouting.

DR LEE: Well, then…?

ELMO: She had a lot to shout about.

DR LEE: I'm sorry. I'm not following.

Pause.

ELMO: And her periods have stopped.

DR LEE: Her periods would have stopped anyway.

Pause.

ELMO: Pongo… Peter is finding the side effects increasingly difficult to live with.

DR LEE: His impotence is temporary.

ELMO: The skin lesions are not responding to treatment.

DR LEE: Because he keeps scratching them.

ELMO: He's finding it hard to concentrate.

DR LEE: That's because of the Valium not the TR14.

ELMO: His motor skills have started to deteriorate.

DR LEE: That's because of the Thorazine not the TR14.

ELMO: I would suggest the killing of the swan was nothing short of disastrous to the TR14 study.

DR LEE: A minor blip only to be expected by a patient prone to psychosis…

ELMO: Up until the swan, Peter…had never betrayed any symptoms of psychosis.

DR LEE: How can you say that? We know very little of his past, he only started remembering himself three months ago. It's quite possible there are very serious manic or psychotic episodes we know nothing about.

ELMO: I don't believe that.

DR LEE: You see Peter as a harmless English eccentric?

ELMO: Not entirely.

DR LEE: With anti-social problems aggravated or provoked by alcohol?

ELMO: Or grief, or loneliness or heightened sensitivity, or surviving on the streets for thirty years…

DR LEE: We know after his mother died he most probably

suffered a complete breakdown.

ELMO: Look, I am observing changes in some of the TR14 volunteers that are causing me concern. Derek was interested in current affairs, a lively debater, now he won't even read a paper.

DR LEE: (*Sarcastically.*) Well, that is worrying.

ELMO: Elaine had a healthy mistrust of doctors; now she seems to view them all as demi-gods.

DR LEE laughs.

When Peter came in here, yes, he was a stroppy pisshead, but I thought underneath all the shit he was probably a really clever bloke, educated…even intellectual. TR14 seems to have put him into a sort of permanent semi-infantile state.

DR LEE: Of course we shouldn't have favourite patients but I've always found Peter particularly endearing.

What *I* have observed in the Test volunteers is that they all seem to be achieving a kind of perfectly enviable state of inner peace.

Pause.

ELMO: Inner peace?

DR LEE: Yes, inner peace.

ELMO: Actually I'm here to tell you that Peter wishes to leave the Centre.

Pause.

I realize in the wake of the swan incident this won't be immediately possible, but my strong advice, and I will be putting this in writing, is that Pongo leaving the centre should be our 'next'.

A long pause.

DR LEE: Absolutely…and I'm much less worried by the swan incident than yourself. If Peter wishes to leave I don't see why we can't try and bring that forward.

Long pause.

You seem surprised.

What did you think I was going to say? That I forbade him leaving, but that would be preposterous…

Pause.

ELMO: I thought he was a psycho.

DR LEE: I never said that.

ELMO: You said he was 'prone to psychosis'. I quote you.

DR LEE: I said it was possible.

ELMO: Probable…that is what I understood.

DR LEE: I said because we didn't have his past history it was quite possible, I quote, I said 'quite possible'.

ELMO: Okay, so if it's quite possible is it fair to release a quite possibly psychotic patient back into the community.

DR LEE: We would have to discuss the…terms and… conditions of his leaving.

ELMO: He's a volunteer. He has to discuss nothing.

DR LEE: I would wish to organise a support system for Peter.

ELMO: Yeah?

DR LEE: There is a community of ex-patients in Cornwall, funded by Pharmaceutica. It's a groundbreaking initiative. They manage independent lives under the detached support of resident Facilitators…

ELMO: A…'useful and fully contributing member of society', I quote you.

DR LEE: Ex-patients cook, clean, shop.

ELMO: 'I would consider anything else an…abject…' I like that word…abject…'an abject failure'.

DR LEE: They work within the community.

ELMO: Cleaning crap off the beach, lollipop men, car park attendants.

DR LEE: Extremely useful work…and they have a skills swap system…

ELMO: You cook scones for me and I'll teach you to line dance.

DR LEE: Exactly…

ELMO: And you think Pongo would be happy, do you?

DR LEE: Yes, Elmo, I think 'Pongo' would be extremely happy, and if you could just stop ranting for half a minute, I think you'd think so too.

Long pause, ELMO paces.

ELMO: May I ask how you would record Pongo's departure in the study notes?

DR LEE: In the spirit of openness that I, myself, initiated at this Centre, of course!

I would record that TR14 had enabled the patient, known as Peter, to be discharged, and that with full support, including financial help, from Pharmaceutica as a gesture of thanks for his invaluable help in the groundbreaking TR14 study, he was able to lead an improved life.

ELMO turns away and laughs.

I can't win with you can I, Elmo? If I refuse to release Peter from the study I am denying him his basic human rights and, until I obtain a section – acting illegally, and if I wholeheartedly support his discharge I'm washing my hands of him, or buying him off, or something even more sinister…and far-fetched.

What should I do? You tell me.

ELMO turns to go.

Elmo, please…you surely realise by now that this is not your average drugs test?

Pause.

ELMO: Isn't it?

DR LEE: No, no it isn't, TR14; the whole package, has… unique expectations put upon it.

Pause.

ELMO: Go on.

DR LEE: The slaughter of those women and children by the horses that night outside the Park was not just a tragic accident, it was an act of criminal barbarism by the Metropolitan Police, and it happened because of an inexcusable nineteenth-century approach to riot patrol and crowd control.

You're aware the protests are happening daily, ships aren't leaving port, town centres are being made impassable, sometimes by just a handful of women. Order has to be kept, Elmo. We cannot allow civil protests to catapult us into full-scale anarchy, but, and this is a very big but, we cannot tear gas school kids, we cannot shoot plastic bullets at babies.

The phone rings. DR LEE picks it up.

Yes. I see. Well, of course it's late but we'll be right there.

Phone down.

How irritating.

Pause.

Peter has just told the nursing auxiliary, that he can no longer see.

4

PONGO seated. He has nodded off. DR LEE and ELMO stand watching him. PONGO snorts, he wakes, he is blind.

PONGO: (*His speech is slightly slurred.*) Have they all gone?

DR LEE: (*Coldly.*) Yes, Peter.

PONGO: And Elmo?

ELMO: I'm here mate.

Pause.

PONGO: So, I've gone blind.

DR LEE: Yes.

PONGO: Because of the drugs.

DR LEE says nothing.

I suppose it's my age isn't it? Making things more difficult.

DR LEE: Possibly.

Pause.

PONGO: Have I botched up the study?

DR LEE: Not in the least.

PONGO: I keep hearing your baby. You bring her into the Centre?

DR LEE: When I can.

PONGO: What's her name?

Pause.

DR LEE: Portia.

PONGO: That's lovely…

You smell of…milk. Mam smelt of… I can't remember…coal?

DR LEE: (*Irritable.*) Look, Peter, it's late and I am very tired and…

PONGO: You're busy; a very busy lady…apparently…and important here in the Centre, they think a lot of you, Pharmaceutica, well at the highest-level…people from the Home Office ring you up…they ask you…questions.

Pause.

You'll be famous after this study…TR14 …

Pause.

DR LEE looks at him.

Elmo…did you know that, Doctor'll be rich and famous.

DR LEE moves away.

Don't leave me.

PONGO stretches out his hand.

Pause.

You know I love you.

Pause.

Can I touch your face? Can I see you as a blind man?

Take my hand.

Pause. DR LEE takes PONGO's hand and puts it to her face.

You are beautiful…

Why are you shaking? Why are you sweating?

Pause. He whispers.

I know.

DR LEE: Sorry.

PONGO: I know it's you; I know you come into my bedroom at night, you stand over me, you open my drawers take out my books, my diary, so you know exactly what I'm thinking.

Long pause, she paces.

DR LEE: I'm not really sure I believe in your blindness.

PONGO: No?

DR LEE: Hysterical blindness, muteness, deafness, paralysis are well documented in the twentieth century psychology as primary controlling behaviour…

PONGO: Dr Lee doesn't think I'm really blind, Elmo?

ELMO: No.

PONGO: She thinks it's…

ELMO: Psychosomatic.

DR LEE: Or maybe you are feigning blindness.

PONGO: Feigning?

DR LEE: Yes, pretending to go blind.

PONGO: Pretending?

DR LEE: It is…

PONGO: Irksome.

DR LEE: Coming as it does so far into the study it…

PONGO: Holds things up.

Pause.

It…comes at a difficult time,

Pause.

it makes things… awkward for you,

Pause.

you could always say I would have gone blind anyway.

DR LEE: (*Aggressive.*) I'm never sure when you're joking, Peter.

PONGO: Tell her, Elmo.

DR LEE looks at ELMO.

DR LEE: You enjoy playing games with us, don't you Peter? You have thought all along that you are cleverer than all of us on the study?

Only I have been aware of this.

PONGO: (*To DR LEE.*) Now you, you see me as a blind man…I'll look quite different.

Pause.

Am I too ugly?…Too old?

Pause.

People touch each other… You'll have to try and get used to it.

DR LEE refuses to touch PONGO.

Please...please.

PONGO reaches out to find her...he grasps her wrist, she is taken by surprise, she tries to pull away, he doesn't let go. She presses a panic button on her wrist, an alarm sounds throughout the Centre. It panics and disorientates PONGO, he freezes. She looks directly into camera.

DR LEE: (*Calmly.*) Security to Room 7a, please.

ELMO: Heh...mate.

PONGO: Is your pussy wet?

Can I see you bra?

ELMO: Let go, let her go.

PONGO: I'm all knob.

DR LEE: Security to room 7a please.

He lets go of her wrist. The alarm continues.

ELMO: That's good Pongo, good lad. Don't be scared.

PONGO: (*Looking into camera.*) I've spoken to The Park People.

DR LEE: When?

PONGO: They come up to the window at night. They whisper. They hold up cards and pictures.

DR LEE: (*To ELMO.*) Is this possible?

ELMO shrugs.

PONGO: What will happen next?

DR LEE: You will lead a pleasant and useful life.

ELMO: (*Under his breath.*) You will become a lollipop man.

PONGO: I want to play jazz trumpet.

I want to have sex.

Running footsteps.

Will the Park people break the windows?

Will they hurt me?

DR LEE: You can accept my word that I will do everything in my power to ensure that does not happen.

PONGO: Will they hurt you? Will they hurt your husband and baby?

Pause.

Will they hurt Portia?

Pause.

DR LEE: They might try.

CCTV. Long distance. Blurred images. Empty Park. Night. Two women stealthily walk across the grass.

5

PONGO's room. The light suggests confinement, even bars, ELMO is standing looking out of a window. He is tense, restless.

PONGO sits. He is shockingly deteriorated. He has dark rings under his eyes. He shakes.

PONGO: Where are the swans?

ELMO: Over the other side of the lake.

PONGO: Where's...? Where's...?

ELMO: I can only see six.

PONGO: Has he left the park then?

ELMO: Maybe.

PONGO: To find another mate?

ELMO: Sometimes, the other swans attack a lone male.

PONGO: Do they?

ELMO: Or drive them away.

PONGO: Poor swan.

Pause.

Did he get my letter?

ELMO: Pongo, swans can't read.

PONGO: I said you should have read it out to him. Will they ever let me out in the Park again?

ELMO: Don't hold your breath.

Purr of passing engine.

What's that?

A great big fucking chauffeur driven Rolls.

PONGO: Who is it?

ELMO: The cops are saluting.

PONGO: Pharmaceutica rule England now, don't they, Elmo?

ELMO: You're a comedian, you know that Pong.

PONGO: Why doesn't Elaine spoon with all the men now?

ELMO: She's found inner peace.

PONGO: Why doesn't Derek argue with everybody anymore?

ELMO: Ditto…

PONGO is with ELMO at the 'window', he moves his head.

What are you seeing now?

PONGO: I don't see things anymore, only light and dark but I don't miss things, and now I see Dr Lee again...

Did I go blind cos I wanked?

ELMO: No.

PONGO: Did I go blind cos I stopped wanking?

ELMO: Are you having us on old son, eh?

You can tell me.

Pause.

It'll be our little secret.

Just between you and me.

Pause.

It's causing a lot of problems.

You know that. Don't you, Pongo. This blindness?

They want to take you off the study. They might even stop the study, close it down, send everyone away.

Footsteps on gravel.

PONGO: They're changing the guard. How many of them?

ELMO: More every day.

PONGO: Knock, knock.

ELMO: Who's there?

PONGO: Boo.

ELMO: Boo who?

PONGO: Don't cry, Elmo, it's all a big joke.

Pause.

You're not doing your act tonight, are you?

ELMO: No.

PONGO: Why?

Pause.

ELMO: Something... funny happened last week.

PONGO: That's good.

ELMO: No, no...something...odd. Something really fucking odd, look...

ELMO paces.

You know, the bra thing in the act that just happened one night and I kept it in, because...well, I don't know, people seemed to like it, they came especially to see that bit, well you would wouldn't you. So last week we get to the bra taking-off bit and this girl stood up. I hadn't noticed her, quiet, young, small, looked a bit of a retard, she got up and she pulled off her top and undid her bra, a little white number, a bit grey actually; a little school girl thing and she just stood, very still with these sticky arms and saggy tits, a little operation scar just under her belly and then she took off her trousers, her knickers, shoes and socks and she just stood there. I mean naked her bony pale veiny little body and somehow it wasn't funny! I mean no-one laughed, no-one and then another woman stood, big woman older and did the same thing, you know took off her clothes and just stood and I was trying to gag through it, turn the situation round but I was starting to sweat...I mean sweat was dripping onto the stage I started to shake. Another stood up and another and they just stood there, staring at me and no-one was laughing just this…wall of silence…

And then the bouncers barged through knocking tables
and drinks, strong arming, and no way was that right
cos they were just people, you know, naked people
and a couple struggled and were pushed to the floor
then dragged out, some were carried over the boy's
shoulders looking…awful like bits of meat and…no-one
was laughing.

Outside it was really cold. I saw the bouncers in a
huddle.

I think the moon shifted and through their legs I saw the
naked girl, the first one who had stood up in the club,
kneeling.

I mean she looked terrified. She tried to scream. One
of the bouncers grabbed her, he put his hand over her
mouth.

I swear to God, Pong, I was so angry, so very, very
angry I wanted to join in, at that moment I wanted to
teach the little bitch the fucking lesson of her friggin'
life.

Teach her to fucking humiliate me.

Teach her to destroy my act.

Little Cunt.

I wanted to ram my cock up her that hard she'd squeal
like a fuckin' stuck pig. I did.

But I didn't do that.

The moon shifted again for a minute, I couldn't see her.

So.

I turned.

I turned, Pongo.

And I ran away.

Long pause. PONGO takes in deep, long breaths, then:

PONGO: (*In a fury, out of the window, to the guards.*) Get out of the Park, do you hear me? Let the people come back!

Under his coat he mimes a gun.

Get out, you fuckers, or I'll shoot. Bang! Bang! Bang!

Pause. ELMO and PONGO are confronted by security guards who have walked up to the window and are peering in.

ELMO: (*Holding hands up.*) Put your hands where they can see them, Pongo.

PONGO does so.

No, look, no, it's okay boys. He's a mad blind man. Look it's okay!

6

ELMO: I turned and walked out into the air. It was cold and there was a curtain of drizzle. In the mist the guards looked like...I don't know ghosts from the future p'raps...or aliens

The ground steamed.

The lake was black and invisible.

And the swans slept, I suppose.

It was so quiet, I could hear myself breathe.

At the Gate.

Flash the ID.

'Shouldn't come this way.'

'Sorry Pal.'

I wonder if she's still there. The handless woman. I can't see her yet. I can see the terrible shabby black-eyed women.

I can smell her, closer…and I gag. It's a sweet, rotting, maggoty smell…

…and to me it's a female sort of smell, an ancient smell.

And then two or three of them shift and I see…the empty deckchair…and I…panic, my heart starts to pound, I pant, I sweat and I start to push the women away, searching and I hear myself calling. Where is she?

7

PONGO sits. He is in complete darkness. DR LEE enters.

PONGO: (*Nervous.*) Who is it?

Pause.

It's you.

DR LEE: Can you see me?

PONGO: Before I only saw light and dark. Now I see shapes.

DR LEE: Well, that's good.

PONGO: The shapes are like monsters. They frighten me.

DR LEE: Do you mind if I switch on the lamp?

PONGO: No.

She does so, she sees PONGO is holding Portia, she gasps.

You mustn't press your panic alarm.

DR LEE: No.

PONGO: She was crying.

DR LEE: Give her to me.

Pause.

PONGO: You're frightened.

DR LEE: Yes, yes I'm very frightened. Give her to me.

PONGO: (*Standing with her tenderly.*) Sssh! You'll wake her.

Pause.

I want a drug that stops me remembering.

DR LEE: I'll get you one. It's easy.

PONGO: Really?

DR LEE: Of course. I'll arrange it.

PONGO: (*Astonished.*) You'd do anything I asked now wouldn't you?

DR LEE: Yes. Yes I'll do anything.

PONGO: Anything?

DR LEE: Yes, only please don't hurt my baby.

Long pause. She breathes unsteadily.

PONGO: Anything.

Pause.

There are things I would like to forget.

DR LEE: I know, I understand, truly I do, there are things I want to forget.

PONGO: What things?

DR LEE: Oh, so many things, just like you, my mother died… Yes…I was…it was sad, so sad…just like you…

PONGO: You're lying.

Pause.

DR LEE: You're right I'm lying...you're right...she divorced my father, remarried, he drank, spent all her money...we had no food, I used to hide under the bed when he came home, once he was drunk, he locked my mother in the bedroom...and kissed me, put his tongue in my mouth, made me feel sick – that's the truth.

Give me my baby, please.

PONGO turns away cradling her.

PONGO: Sssh!

Pause.

DR LEE: My father tried to kill himself. He overdosed, survived and died in hospital of kidney failure on New Year's Eve looking forward to Spring...isn't that terrible, Peter? Isn't that a terrible thing? I'm not British. Do you know that?

PONGO shakes his head.

I'm Czech. I watched the Russian tanks rolling in perched on his shoulders. No, there's so many things you don't know about me. Please, Peter, give me Portia, please.

He pulls away cradling her.

PONGO: She's asleep. You mustn't wake her.

Pause. She breathes deeply. She is distracted in a kind of panicked shock.

DR LEE: We were told the Russian soldiers were...raping our girls...course I didn't know what it meant, I was five, raping our girls and beating up their husbands, so...they'd got us a 'live one' us...we, a Russian soldier

at the school. It was night and dark...the first time I
ever remember being out in the dark. My father took a
stick for himself, large, curved...and gave me Grandpa's
walking stick with a warm brass handle, an acorn,
I remember and I felt so...important, so grown up
carrying Grandpa's best walking stick.

Inside a candle flickered, we were in the hall where the
big kids danced in their vests I remember...

She can hardly breathe.

...I remember ropes and an old vaulting horse and then
I saw him crouched in the corner, a boy that's all, a boy
in a Russian uniform...his nose was bloody, someone
had tied an orange handkerchief very tight round his
mouth...

She gasps.

...an orange spotted handkerchief.

And his eyes....his eyes...

All around men and women...children...us...no one
spoke...no one...I remember

She can hardly breathe.

The thud...stick on bone, the men sweating with the
effort of each blow, women's eyes, aunties, neighbours,
shiny with...hatred...Peter...there...there...the knee,
the head.

Then...they...we, dragged him out into the black
playground, I remember where the big children played
hopscotch, it smelt of wild rose.

Someone, a large man I didn't know with muddy boots
and bitten nails, threw the rope from the gym round
the old knotty tree and then put a loop round the boys
neck. Standing there...he was like my mother tying my

father's necktie for work.

Then…then…

A sudden jerk.

They laughed, the tiny children, I remember, they laughed at the puppet man and his funny jerky dance.

I didn't laugh, Peter.

He smelt of shit, blood bubbled from the gash in his face, his eyes were blind, blind Peter, I wonder what he saw in his last minutes.

Mama, he said.

Pause. She breaks down, sobbing.

So, you see, Peter, you see, I want to forget his cry, I want to forget the eyes of…them…us… Don't hurt Portia, please don't hurt her…

PONGO: (*Looking down at the sleeping baby.*) I've never held a baby before, never in my life.

DR LEE is silent, she looks at them.

She's so small and she's so warm, like a little…like a little…she's perfect.

DR LEE: You can see her?

PONGO: Yes.

DR LEE: You were pretending to be blind?

PONGO: Yes.

Do you believe in God?

DR LEE: No.

PONGO: Mam didn't believe in God.

Shall I tell you a secret?

'Course I kept it from Mam.

I believed in God.

I believed God was a Stork.

I believed God was a pink Flamingo.

I believed God was a Swan.

But I was wrong.

I am God.

Pause. He hands Portia back to DR LEE.

You see, mam was right all along.

I forgive you.

I forgive them.

CCTV. Blurred images. PONGO in restraint jacket in a ferocious struggle with guards. Only partly in shot – DR LEE, ELMO stand. He is being kept from PONGO. He says: 'No, let him go. You don't understand.'

Blackout.

8

Lights up slowly. PONGO seated, his back to the audience. He is not lit. ELMO stands and reads the letter

ELMO: (*Reading a letter.*) Dear Peter, she puts Peter in quotation marks, I was very surprised to get your letter and sorry to hear of all your troubles, my memory isn't what it was either.

However, if you are Elizabeth Harrison's son, born in 1928, 3 Nut Street, West Gorton, Manchester, your real name is Gabriel. Why your mother chose such an unusual name I don't know. To my knowledge she wasn't religious. I'm not surprised you forgot it, you were teased that much, because of it.

You were a pretty clever little boy and the apple of your mother's eye.

PONGO starts to do a good impression of a jazz trumpet. Soft at first and then louder.

One thing that made me laugh. You mention a great brick wall. The houses in Nut Street backed onto Belle Vue Zoo, over the wall was the exotic bird pond and beyond that the lions and tigers.

We used to hear the squawks and roars at feeding time, and you and I used to have a chuckle about who was eating who.

I hope this helps.

God Bless.

Your friend Annie Ezard.

9

Jazz trumpet.

PONGO. ELMO. DR LEE.

Three months later. Lights slowly up. PONGO's chair turns around. Lights slowly up. PONGO sits, utterly changed, vacant, staring. His mouth open. He slobbers, he wears a bib. ELMO attends. DR LEE wears an expensive and glamorous business suit, heels and smart hair.

DR LEE: Now, what's all this about Gabriel?

Pause.

ELMO: He's stopped speaking.

DR LEE: Since when?

ELMO: A few days ago.

DR LEE: He's stopped speaking to *you*, Elmo (*She smiles.*)
but of course he'll speak to me.

*She lifts PONGO's eyelids, points a small torch in his
eyes.*

I hear you've stopped reading Gabriel...

And writing.

That's a shame.

You had a beautiful hand.

I remember.

Feeling his glands.

What about your jigsaws, Gabriel?

(*To ELMO.*) Does he acknowledge anything or anyone?

ELMO: A few seconds' eye contact sometimes, that's all.

DR LEE: But he eats?

ELMO: Only if I feed him.

DR LEE: (*Sighing.*) Raise your left arm for me Gabriel.

Pause.

Your left arm.

PONGO does nothing.

Flex your fingers for me, will you?

Pause. He does nothing.

Blink, Gabriel, blink twice at me.

(*To ELMO.*) Does he go out at all, now?

ELMO: It's difficult...

DR LEE: Why?

ELMO: He won't cooperate. He makes himself…stiff, difficult to move.

Pause.

DR LEE: (*To PONGO.*) I have been talking about you with my colleagues, other doctors here at the Centre, also I work at a teaching hospital and I've shown them some film of you…so you see, you're quite the film star, Gabriel.

I have decided…

Pause.

I have decided…to make significant changes to your medication.

She pats his hand.

You're lucky to have such a devoted nurse looking after you… Thank you Elmo.

She moves away. ELMO races after her.

Yes?

ELMO: These changes.

They'll stop the deterioration will they…any further deterioration?

DR LEE: I fervently hope so, Elmo.

She tries to go.

ELMO: (*Chasing her.*) So there is a chance that he will get… back?

DR LEE: Back?

ELMO: More or less back to the way he was.

DR LEE: That's a strange question coming from a

professional. It is surely not in anybody's interest, not even Gabriel's, that he return to a state of possibly dangerous psychosis.

She goes, he stands staring after her.

ELMO: (*Angrily to PONGO.*) What's the matter with you, eh? Sitting there like a vedge? Showing me up. Don't think I don't know you're doing this on purpose, aren't you, eh…aren't you?

Don't come that, you can hear me all right. You can hear the fucking tea trolley…and you could speak if you wanted…you've a big enough gob on you, it's only moving your chin up and down.

Fighting back tears he takes a damp cloth and tenderly wipes his mouth.

You looked smart for her, though I say it myself.

He brushes PONGO's hair with his hands. He brings a bowl of water, a flannel, soap, a towel and his pyjamas. ELMO starts to undress him, getting him ready for bed. It is a practiced routine, known to both of them, without acknowledging his presence, PONGO cooperates with the procedure. ELMO starts by taking off his shirt.

You're never going to pull a chick looking like that.

He is giving him a skilled blanket bath, washing his face, neck, upper body, patting him dry, a few puffs of talc. It is done with immense love and tenderness. He puts on pyjama top.

Knock, knock.

Who's there?

Aldus.

Aldus who?

Aldus fuss over little old me.

ELMO kneels, washes his feet.

Knock, knock.

Who's there?

Bascilli.

Bascilli who?

Don't Bascilli.

ELMO hands PONGO a towel.

Ermine for your crown jewels. Trews down.

PONGO whimpers.

Well wash yourself.

He hands him a flannel.

Tenderly.

Come on…give yourself a rub down!

You want to do it. See water's nice and warm!

Come on!

Pause.

Sadly.

Well, don't complain then!

Bottoms up!

Under the towel. ELMO washes PONGO, removing 'nappy', replacing it.

Knock, knock.

Who's there?

Britches.

Britches who?

London britches falling down.

CCTV. From above. PONGO lying down, full length. CCTV images projected throughout scene.

10

DR LEE, ELMO and PONGO stand facing audience.

ELMO: 10:09 Injection started. Facial tics, twitching fingers.

10:12 Injection ended.

10:15 Sweating profusely, restless, has to be restrained by nurse wild flailing of arms.

10:22 Respirations sterterous [sic.] 32 / min pulse 120 / min.

10:25 Neck position suggests opisthonos.

10:26 Extremities held rigidly, pupils moderately dilated and do not respond to light corneal, reflex intact.

Click and whirr… CCTV-close up image of PONGO's face.

Live.

PONGO: She's been dead, oh, years. A hard brown ring appears in the toilet bowl. It's mid-summer and a heat wave…

…and at night I can't sleep for the howling of the big cats, the lions, tigers and leopards pacing to and fro in front the bars of their cages, through the night, to and fro, lifting there heads to the moon, yowling and baring their orange fangs.

One night I get up, I don't know why, down the stairs

and the threadbare rose carpet past Mam's old room, through the scullery, the back door, into the yard.

And there it is

there

stretched out on the brick wall, just above the bins. Its green eyes flashing in the dark like Kryptonite.

A panther.

Huge, sleek, black

and so fierce.

Slowly, oh, so slowly

one foot and then another I creep over the cobbles, past the stinking carsey

my heart plays jazz trumpet.

I hold out my hand trying to touch her soft sleek head.

Trying.

Trying to touch…

ELMO: 10:32 Profuse sweating continued. Frothing at mouth cyanotic.

10:33 Continued sterterous [sic.] respiration 28 / min irregular.

10:34 Jaw clenched. Generalized rigidity, neck, arms, legs.

10:42 Small random movements of arms and legs.

10:47 Movements cease.

10:49 Patient becomes calmer.

10:54 Temperature normal.

10:57 Good colour.

11:02 Breathing steady.

(*To DR LEE.*) I think I owe you an apology.

DR LEE: (*Engrossed in making notes in her palm top.*) Really? What for?

ELMO: Well, the Cornwall idea. The community of ex-patients.

DR LEE: (*Distracted.*) Oh, yes.

ELMO: Well, I've been giving it some thought...a great deal of thought and I really think it is a good idea, I mean I think he might be happy there.

DR LEE: (*Still engrossed in notes.*) 'Course he's not been very well, has he? Not for a long time now?

ELMO: No.

DR LEE: And he was hardly in the best of shape when he turned up at the Centre.

ELMO: No, but...

DR LEE: We mustn't have unrealistic expectations.

ELMO: I...I don't know what you mean.

Click and whirr...image of PONGO's eye, wide expressionless.

11:47 Slight frothing at mouth.

11:52 Intermittently generalized rigidity.

11:57 Lapsing into coma, still restless.

12:07 Becoming cyanotic, respiration rapid and sterterous.

12:31 Quiet deep coma.

Pause.

Click and whirr…image freezes. Lights out on live PONGO.

Pongo is pronounced dead at 12:46.

ELMO stands he is in shock. He breathes unsteadily.

DR LEE: (*Softly.*) Of course, it is a tragedy. Peter, I mean Gabriel was never the easiest of patients.

She smiles.

But that was what made our study, the work, our work together, so challenging and so rewarding.

Pause.

I remember the day he came in, I had never, never in my life seen, or…or…smelt anything like it. He blocked the drains in the men's shower room I know that.

And then this wonderful human being started to emerge…so articulate, a clever man with a wonderful sense of humour…and, well, a poetic soul, I thought. He thought he'd got us sussed, I'm sure.

Pause.

It's quite without precedent but I'd like to do something in his memory. What do you think Elmo? What about a plaque by the lake or a bench with his name on. I think he'd like that.

Softly.

ELMO: … (*Tears roll down ELMO's face.*) Your work has been exemplorary…exemplorary.

CCTV. Click and whirr. A lone figure runs across parkland in the dark. Click and whirr. Another camera takes up image. It is ELMO.

11

ELMO: (*Panting, breathless.*) Halfway across the parkland
I see them, with their banners. And they are creeping,
silent as ghosts.

They spy me, somehow, we stop.

A sharp voice from the dark.

'He's one of them.'

Pointing to my coat,

'See, Pharmaceutica.'

'We have proof that in that building…'

In the darkness a finger points to the Centre.

'…you are conducting illegal and inhumane
experiments on vulnerable human beings, homeless
people, the mentally ill, the disabled, in order to
successfully engineer chemical weapons to be used in
civil insurrection and armed conflict.'

'We have proof,'

shouts another.

'We have the film.'

And then I see her, at the very front of course, in the
middle.

She's taller than I thought and straighter. Her hair's
beginning to grow back. She holds her bloody
bandaged stumps in front of her…like a shield.

I walk towards her…my feet squelching in the wet grass
far away, the screech of a great bird, the women move
in front and I hear her say in a loud clear voice…

'No, leave him.'

…and we face each other and for the first time, for the very first time, I look into her eyes. I don't know what I expected.

Tears? A soft, wet, universal fathomless sadness – Grief! Which is dry and scratchy? Or shock… Perhaps?

The far away look that I suppose passes for madness in women.

That wasn't what I saw in the eyes of the Handless Woman. That wasn't it at all.

What I saw…

What I saw…that night.

Was a savage, bleeding and biting.

Anger!

12

DR LEE in her smart suit addresses the audience. Across the stage a huge banner – PHARMACEUTICA – WAGING PEACE.

DR LEE: As a very small child I remember watching the old film footage of the bombing of Dresden, Coventry, Berlin, London. The nightmare mushroom cloud and the horrific images of human suffering that came out of Hiroshima and Nagasaki have burnt themselves into our collective unconsciousness; they quite simply have defined the twentieth century.

And now, once again, the old nightmare. Our

young soldiers, men and women, engage in another heroic struggle, in a far off land, against tyranny and oppression.

If, like me, you believe that war sometimes is inevitable. That there will always be causes in the long human story that are worth fighting, passionately, for; it will come as no surprise when I say this study has been the defining moment of my working life.

I have a baby daughter, she is not yet one year old, because of our work... The Ministry of Defence Non Lethal Weapons Directorate, the military research scientists, the psycho-pharmaceutical team, the psychiatric team, the social scientists and the legion of professional healthcare workers who enable the study on simply every level, because of all our work, it is possible my daughter's generation, her children and her children's children will never again live under the threat of world annihilation.

At last after five decades of study and research, Pharmaceutica, and I'd like to thank representatives from our mother company in the US for joining us today, have successfully engineered, the first wholly effective, mind altering, peace inducing chemical weapon, a calmative for use against hostile civilians, terrorist organizations, counter insurgence and military operations. Never again will cities or civilisations be needlessly destroyed; never again will innocent lives be lost under the obscenity that is 'collateral damage'.

Ladies and Gentlemen, it is with great pride I announce the launch of Tranqton and with it, the birth of modern humane warfare.

Huge applause, cheering.

13

ELMO: 'How many guards?'

She speaks to me.

We creep together, myself, the Handless Woman and her silent army across the soft grass.

Hundreds I say.

The best place of entry is the conservatory that'll give us direct access to the bedrooms and laboratories beyond.

'We mustn't frighten the…'

Volunteers? I say.

'No!

We are going to set them free.'

Knock, knock.

Who's there?

I see him everywhere…under a tree, a passing cloud…a swan takes flight from the lake.

Ahead now we see the guards.

Are those guns?

She says.

Flame throwers?

Is it tear gas?

They're wearing helmets.

I haven't seen those before.

The Park becomes the Centre, there's no walls, fences, ditches, tripwires.

That was their cunning.

Then

psst!…

from all around

psst!

Like someone's taken the air out of the world…

Psst!

Some saw a faint mist, I mistook it for breath…

Psst!

At first…a slight tingling in fingers and toes…you stop, it's not that you can't move…your muscles relax, like after a long hot bath, for a split second the world blurs, you rub your eyes.

Then,

then,

I hear myself say.

What now?

What next?

The End.